INTRODUCTION

Welcome to "How to Become a Master Prompter," a comprehensive guide that will equip you with the knowledge and skills to excel at prompt writing for AI platforms. In this book, we will explore the fundamentals of prompt writing, delve into the intricacies of AI platforms, and provide valuable insights to help you craft engaging and effective prompts. Prompt writing for AI platforms has become a significant field as the demand for AI-generated content continues to rise. AI platforms rely heavily on well-crafted prompts to generate coherent and meaningful responses. As a prompt writer, your role is vital in shaping the AI's ability to produce accurate and relevant content. In this book, we will start by laying the foundation with Chapter 1, where we will explore the basics of prompt writing. Understanding the core principles and techniques will help you create prompts that elicit the desired responses from AI models. In Chapter 2, we will dive into the world of AI platforms. This chapter aims to provide you with a comprehensive understanding of how AI platforms function, their capabilities, and limitations. Understanding the underlying technology will enable you to optimize your prompt writing process. Crafting engaging prompts is an art form that will be explored in Chapter 3. The ability to captivate and evoke the desired response from AI models is crucial. We will explore various strategies and techniques to make your prompts more engaging and effective. Building a strong prompt library is the focus of Chapter 4. A well-curated prompt library provides a diverse range of options, allowing you to generate a variety of responses. We will discuss how to organize and expand your prompt library to enhance the quality of AI-generated content. Prompt structures play a significant role in shaping the output of

AI models. In Chapter 5, we will delve into different prompt structures and their impact on responses. By mastering prompt structures, you can steer AI models towards generating desired outcomes. Analyzing prompt responses will be the focus of Chapter 6. Understanding and evaluating the generated responses is crucial to refine and optimize your prompts. We will explore techniques to analyze and interpret prompt responses effectively. Chapter 7 will guide you on enhancing prompt diversity. AI models are sensitive to the input they receive, and by diversifying prompts, you can foster creativity and avoid repetitive or biased outputs. Prompt writing comes with its own set of challenges, which will be addressed in Chapter 8. From handling ambiguous queries to managing user expectations, we will provide strategies to overcome common prompt challenges. Prompt performance optimization will be discussed in Chapter 9. By applying optimization techniques, you can enhance the efficiency and accuracy of AI-generated content. Finally, in Chapter 10, we will explore advanced prompt writing techniques and tips. This chapter will equip you with additional tools and strategies to take your prompt writing skills to the next level. Whether you are an aspiring prompt writer or already experienced in the field, "How to Become a Master Prompter" will serve as an invaluable resource to enhance your prompt writing skills. Let's embark on this journey together and unlock the true potential of AI-generated content.

The Basics of Prompt Writing

Prompt writing is a fundamental skill for those seeking to become a master prompter. It involves crafting clear and concise instructions that effectively communicate the desired outcome to an AI platform. In this chapter, we will explore the essential elements of prompt writing and provide valuable tips to help you enhance your skills in this area.

Why are Prompts Important?

Prompts act as the foundation for any AI-generated response. They serve as the instructions given to the AI model, guiding it towards producing the desired output. Well-written prompts enable the AI to understand the context, generate coherent responses, and provide valuable information.

The Key Components of a Prompt

A well-crafted prompt consists of several key components: 1. Intent: Clearly specify the objective or desired outcome of the prompt. This helps the AI model understand the purpose behind the request. For example, if you want the AI to generate a creative story, explicitly mention it in the prompt. 2. Context: Provide necessary background information to set the context for the AI model. This could include details about the characters, setting, or any relevant plot points. The more specific and relevant the context, the better the AI's response will be. 3. Instructions: Clearly state the task or question you want the AI to focus on. Be precise and specific in your instructions to avoid ambiguity. This helps the AI understand the exact information or action you expect from it. 4. Examples: Including examples or sample responses can provide additional clarity and help the AI model understand the desired output. Showcasing a few examples of the expected format or content can guide the AI's creativity.

Tips for Effective Prompt Writing

Here are some tips to improve your prompt writing skills: 1. Be clear and concise: Use simple and straightforward language in your prompts. Avoid unnecessary jargon or complexity that may confuse the AI model. The more clarity you provide, the better the AI's response will be. 2. Use specific instructions: Instead of asking open-ended questions, provide specific instructions that guide the AI's response. For example, instead of asking, "What do you think about XYZ?", ask, "Provide three advantages of XYZ." 3. Experiment with different phrasings: Language models may respond differently to slightly different prompts. Experiment with various phrasings to achieve the desired output. 4. Avoid biased phrasing: Be cautious about using prompts that may unintentionally encourage biased or discriminatory responses from the AI model. Ensure inclusivity and fairness in your prompts. By mastering the basics of prompt writing, you lay a strong foundation for becoming an adept prompter. The next chapter will delve into understanding AI platforms and their role in prompt-driven interactions.

CHAPTER 2: UNDERSTANDING AI PLATFORMS

In this chapter, we will delve into the intricate world of AI platforms and explore the key concepts and components that prompt writers need to understand. From familiarizing yourself with the fundamentals to exploring the various types of AI platforms available, this chapter will equip you with the necessary knowledge to navigate and harness the power of these platforms effectively.

The Basics of AI Platforms

To become a master prompter, it is essential to have a solid understanding of AI platforms. AI platforms serve as the foundation on which prompt writers create engaging and interactive content. These platforms incorporate advanced algorithms and machine learning techniques to process vast amounts of data and generate meaningful responses.

Types of AI Platforms

There are several types of AI platforms, each with its unique capabilities and applications. Some platforms are designed for specific industries or purposes, while others offer more general functionalities. Understanding the different types of AI platforms will enable you to identify the most suitable ones for your prompt writing needs.

OpenAI's GPT-3

One of the most prominent AI platforms in recent years is OpenAI's GPT-3 (Generative Pre-trained Transformer 3). GPT-3 is a state-of-the-art language model capable of understanding and generating human-like text. It has been widely adopted by various industries and has revolutionized the way prompt writers create content.

The Role of Prompt Writers

As a prompt writer, it is crucial to comprehend how AI platforms operate and the role you play in the process. You are responsible for crafting prompts that provide the necessary context and guidance for the AI model to generate relevant and coherent responses. By understanding the capabilities and limitations of AI platforms, you can optimize your prompt writing strategies and achieve desired outcomes.

Collaborating with AI Platforms

Successful prompt writing involves a collaborative effort between prompt writers and AI platforms. By exploring and experimenting with different AI platforms, you can acquire valuable insights and techniques that enhance your prompt writing skills. This chapter will guide you on how to effectively collaborate with AI platforms and maximize their potential in generating compelling responses.

Chapter Summary

Understanding AI platforms is vital for prompt writers seeking to master their craft. By grasping the basic principles, exploring different types of platforms, and recognizing your role in the process, you can harness the power of AI platforms to create engaging and impactful prompts. In the following chapters, we will delve deeper into the techniques and strategies of prompt writing, building upon the foundation of understanding AI platforms. With this knowledge, you will be well-equipped to excel in the world of prompt writing for AI platforms.

CHAPTER 3: CRAFTING ENGAGING PROMPTS

The Importance of Engaging Prompts

Crafting engaging prompts is a crucial skill for prompt writers on AI platforms. The quality of the prompt directly impacts the responses generated by the model. An engaging prompt captures the attention of the AI model and inspires it to generate a creative and accurate response. In this chapter, we will explore various techniques and strategies to create prompts that grab the AI's attention and elicit compelling and informative responses.

Understanding the AI Model

Before diving into crafting engaging prompts, it is essential to understand how the AI model processes and interprets information. AI models like OpenAI's GPT-3 have a vast amount of knowledge but require specific instructions to generate coherent responses. By understanding the underlying architecture and functions of the model, prompt writers can optimize their prompts to elicit desired outcomes.

Clarity and Specificity

When creating prompts, clarity and specificity are paramount. Clearly defining the desired outcome or information required from the AI model helps guide its response. Vague or ambiguous prompts may lead to inaccurate or irrelevant answers. By providing specific instructions and context, prompt writers can ensure that the generated responses align with their objectives.

Establishing Context

Context plays a vital role in generating meaningful responses. Providing necessary background information in the prompt allows the AI model to comprehend the desired scope and context of the response. By setting clear boundaries and providing relevant context, prompt writers can guide the AI model to generate accurate and relevant answers.

Using Examples and Analogies

Examples and analogies are powerful tools in crafting engaging prompts. By presenting relatable scenarios or comparisons, prompt writers can help the AI model understand complex concepts and generate more accurate responses. Including real-life examples or using familiar analogies enables the AI model to draw connections and provide insightful information.

Asking Open-Ended Questions

Prompt writers can encourage creativity and explore diverse perspectives by formulating open-ended questions. Open-ended prompts unleash the AI model's imagination and encourage it to generate unique responses. These types of prompts go beyond simple factual answers, allowing for more in-depth and thought-provoking responses.

Personalizing the Prompt

Adding a personalized touch to the prompts can enhance engagement and generate more personalized responses. By incorporating specific details or personal preferences within the prompt, prompt writers can influence the AI model to generate responses tailored to a particular individual or situation.

Experimentation and Iteration

Crafting engaging prompts often involves experimentation and iteration. Prompt writers should not hesitate to try different approaches, rephrase their prompts, or adjust their instructions to achieve the desired outcomes. Through continuous refinement and adaptation, prompt writers can enhance their skills and achieve greater success in generating compelling prompts.

Conclusion

Crafting engaging prompts is an art that prompt writers can master with practice and a deep understanding of the AI model's capabilities. By ensuring clarity, providing context, using examples, asking open-ended questions, personalizing prompts, and embracing experimentation, prompt writers can create prompts that captivate the AI model's attention and deliver valuable and engaging responses. In the next chapter, we will delve into building a robust prompt library to enhance the prompt writing process.

CHAPTER 4: BUILDING A STRONG PROMPT LIBRARY

Building a strong prompt library is an essential aspect of becoming a master prompter. A well-curated prompt library not only saves time and effort but also ensures consistent and high-quality outputs from AI platforms. In this chapter, we will explore various strategies and tips for creating a robust prompt library to maximize the effectiveness of your prompt writing.

1. Identify the Objectives

Before diving into building a prompt library, it is crucial to identify the objectives and goals you want to achieve. Consider the specific needs of the AI platform you are working with and the type of prompts that yield the best results. This will help you create prompts that align with the platform's capabilities and maximize the output quality.

2. Cater to Different Use Cases

To create a versatile prompt library, it is essential to cater to different use cases. Understand the various categories or scenarios where prompts are commonly used and develop prompts accordingly. For example, prompts for customer support scenarios will differ from prompts used for creative writing or technical problem-solving.

3. Use Templates

Using templates can significantly streamline the process of creating prompts. Develop a set of template prompts that can be easily modified to fit different use cases. Templates provide a starting point and ensure consistency in prompt structure and style. They also serve as a reference for future prompt creation.

4. Leverage Previous Prompts

As you gain experience as a prompt writer, you will accumulate a collection of previously used prompts. Review these prompts regularly and identify the ones that have yielded excellent results. Repurpose and modify these prompts to create new variations that can be added to your prompt library. Learning from past successes can enhance the overall quality of your prompts.

5. Include Prompts for Diverse Inputs

To create a comprehensive prompt library, include prompts that cater to diverse inputs. Consider prompts that encourage creativity, critical thinking, problem-solving, and emotional responses. By incorporating prompts that cover a wide range of inputs, you increase the chances of obtaining varied and meaningful outputs from the AI model.

6. Organize and Categorize

Organizing your prompt library in a structured manner can greatly enhance efficiency. Categorize prompts based on different topics, use cases, or target audiences. This way, when you need a prompt for a specific situation, you can easily locate and retrieve the relevant prompt without wasting time searching through a cluttered library.

7. Regularly Update and Refresh

Prompt libraries should not remain stagnant. The AI landscape is constantly evolving, and new techniques and strategies emerge over time. It is crucial to stay updated with the latest advancements and incorporate them into your prompt library.

Regularly refreshing your prompt collection ensures that you are utilizing the most effective and efficient prompts. Building a strong prompt library requires time, effort, and a constant drive for improvement. By implementing these strategies and continually refining your prompt collection, you will enhance your prompt writing skills and achieve outstanding results on AI platforms. Next, in Chapter 5, we will delve into the intricacies of mastering prompt structures and how to create prompts that elicit the desired responses from AI models.

CHAPTER 5: MASTERING PROMPT STRUCTURES

In this chapter, we will delve into the art of mastering prompt structures. Crafting well-structured prompts is essential for prompt writers to effectively communicate with AI platforms and elicit accurate and meaningful responses. A carefully constructed prompt can significantly influence the quality and relevance of the AI-generated output.

Understanding Prompt Structures

To master prompt structures, it is important to understand their components and how they interact with the AI model. A prompt typically consists of the following elements:

1. Instruction:

The instruction guides the AI model on what task or information is expected. It provides a clear direction for the AI system to focus on and generate relevant responses accordingly.

2. Context:

Including relevant context in your prompt helps the AI model understand the specific scenario or topic you are referring to. Providing contextual information ensures that the AI-generated response aligns with the desired context.

3. Examples:

Including examples in your prompt can help the AI model better understand the desired output. By providing clear and concise examples, you can guide the AI towards generating responses that are similar to the examples provided.

4. Follow-up Questions:

Prompt structures can also include follow-up questions to further guide the AI model. These questions serve to prompt the AI to dive deeper into a specific topic or provide additional information based on the initial response.

Designing Effective Prompt Structures

To design effective prompt structures, you should consider the following tips:

1. Be Clear and Concise:

Ensure that your prompt is straightforward and unambiguous. Avoid using jargon or complex language that might confuse the AI model. Clearly state what you are looking for in a concise manner.

2. Establish Context:

Begin your prompt by providing relevant context to the AI model. This context will help the AI better understand the desired outcome and generate more appropriate responses.

3. Use Specific Examples:

Including specific examples in your prompts can help the AI model grasp the desired output more effectively. By providing concrete examples, you can guide the AI towards producing responses that align with the desired tone, style, or content.

4. Ask Open-ended Questions:

To encourage the AI model to provide detailed and comprehensive responses, ask open-ended questions within your prompts. Open-ended questions prompt the AI to elaborate and provide more information rather than just a simple answer.

5. Experiment and Iterate:

Don't be afraid to experiment with different prompt structures and variations. Test different approaches, rephrase your prompts, and iterate based on the results. Continuous experimentation allows you to refine your prompt structures and improve the quality of the generated responses.

Summary

Mastering prompt structures is crucial for any prompt writer looking to maximize the potential of AI platforms. By understanding the key elements of a prompt and following effective design principles, prompt writers can elicit accurate and relevant responses from AI models. Remember the importance of being clear, providing context, using examples, asking open-ended questions, and embracing experimentation. Developing proficiency in prompt structures will significantly enhance your effectiveness as a prompt writer and improve the overall performance of AI-generated output. Please note that the content of this chapter focuses on the fundamental concepts and techniques related to mastering prompt structures, without specifically delving into the OpenAI's GPT-3 model or other specific AI platforms.

CHAPTER 6: ANALYZING PROMPT RESPONSES

Analyzing prompt responses is a crucial step for prompt writers on AI platforms. It enables them to assess the effectiveness of their prompts, understand the behavior of the AI model, and make any necessary improvements. In this chapter, we will delve into the process of analyzing prompt responses and explore various techniques to optimize results.

Understanding Prompt Evaluation Metrics

When analyzing prompt responses, it is essential to have a clear understanding of the evaluation metrics used by the AI platform. OpenAI's GPT-3, for example, employs metrics such as perplexity, BLEU score, and human evaluation. Perplexity measures the model's confidence in its predictions, while BLEU score assesses the similarity between the generated text and a reference text. Human evaluation involves obtaining feedback from human reviewers to gauge the quality and relevance of the generated responses.

Establishing Evaluation Criteria

Prompt writers need to establish their own evaluation criteria based on the desired outcomes. This can include factors like relevancy, coherence, clarity, creativity, and overall usefulness of the generated responses. By setting clear evaluation criteria, prompt writers can focus on specific areas for improvement and tailor their prompts accordingly.

Reviewing and Annotating Responses

After receiving prompt responses from the AI model, it is important to review and annotate them systematically. Prompt writers should evaluate each response against their established evaluation criteria. This process involves identifying strengths and weaknesses in the generated text and making note of any errors, inconsistencies, or irrelevant content. By annotating responses, prompt writers can gain valuable insights into the performance of their prompts and identify patterns or trends.

Iterative Feedback Loop

Analyzing prompt responses should not be a one-time task but rather an iterative process. Prompt writers should use the insights gained from previous analyses to refine their prompts and improve future iterations. This feedback loop allows them to constantly learn and adapt their approach to generate more accurate and effective responses.

Collaboration with AI Platforms

Prompt writers can also collaborate with AI platforms to further enhance prompt analysis. By sharing feedback and discussing challenges faced during prompt analysis, prompt writers can contribute to the development and improvement of the AI model. Open communication and collaboration between prompt writers and AI platforms can lead to a more robust and accurate prompt generation process. In conclusion, analyzing prompt responses is an essential component of prompt writing on AI platforms. By understanding evaluation metrics, establishing clear criteria, reviewing and annotating responses, maintaining an iterative feedback loop, and collaborating with AI platforms, prompt writers can continuously improve their prompts and optimize the results generated by AI models. Next, in Chapter 7, we will explore techniques for enhancing prompt diversity to bring more variety and creativity to prompt writing on AI platforms.

CHAPTER 7: ENHANCING PROMPT DIVERSITY

In the world of prompt writing for AI platforms, it is not only important to create engaging and effective prompts, but also to ensure diversity in the prompts you provide. Enhancing prompt diversity plays a significant role in improving the AI model's ability to generate diverse and inclusive responses. This chapter will explore various techniques and strategies to enhance prompt diversity and create more versatile outputs.

The Importance of Prompt Diversity

Prompt diversity refers to the variety of prompts that are used to train and fine-tune AI models. By incorporating a wide range of prompts, prompt writers can help the AI system understand and respond to different perspectives, cultural nuances, and unique scenarios. This allows the AI model to generate more comprehensive and diverse responses, catering to a wider range of user needs.

Techniques for Enhancing Prompt Diversity

1. **Consider Different Perspectives:** While crafting prompts, prompt writers should strive to incorporate a diverse range of perspectives. By including prompts that cover various demographics, cultures, and experiences, the AI model becomes more attuned to different viewpoints. 2. **Include Multicultural**

and **Multilingual Prompts:** Incorporating prompts in different languages and cultures can help the AI model understand and respond to a broader user base. By including prompts that represent different cultural contexts, the AI model becomes more capable of generating culturally sensitive responses. 3. **Capture Niche and Specialized Topics:** To ensure prompt diversity, it is crucial to include prompts that cover niche or specialized topics. This allows AI models to generate accurate and informative responses in specific domains, catering to users with specialized needs. 4. **Experiment with Prompt Structures:** Prompt writers should experiment with different prompt structures and formats to encourage diverse responses from the AI model. By varying the way prompts are presented, such as using multiple-choice options or providing specific constraints, prompt diversity can be further enhanced. 5. **Collaborate with a Diverse Team:** Working with a diverse team of prompt writers can greatly contribute to enhancing prompt diversity. Different perspectives, cultural backgrounds, and areas of expertise within the team can enrich the diversity of prompts generated. 6. **Keep Up with Current Events and Trends:** Staying up-to-date with current events, trends, and cultural discussions is crucial in prompt writing. Including prompts that reflect current societal issues and conversations helps the AI model stay relevant and generate responses that align with the changing landscape.

Measuring and Evaluating Prompt Diversity

To assess and measure prompt diversity effectively, prompt writers can use a combination of qualitative and quantitative approaches. Some techniques include: 1. **Qualitative Evaluation:** Prompt writers can review the prompts in their library to ensure representation from different perspectives, cultures, and domains. They can assess the inclusion of relevant and trending topics to maximize prompt diversity. 2. **Quantitative Evaluation:** Analyzing the output generated by the AI model can provide insights into prompt diversity. Examining the distribution of responses across different demographics, themes, or languages can help identify any gaps in prompt diversity.

Conclusion

Enhancing prompt diversity is vital for prompt writers on AI platforms. By considering different perspectives, including multicultural prompts, capturing niche topics, experimenting with prompt structures, collaborating with a diverse team, and staying updated with current events, prompt writers can ensure inclusive and versatile responses from AI models. Measuring and evaluating prompt diversity using qualitative and quantitative methods helps prompt writers continuously improve their prompt libraries and optimize AI-generated outputs.

CHAPTER 8: DEALING WITH COMMON PROMPT CHALLENGES

Prompt writing on AI platforms can come with its fair share of challenges. In this chapter, we'll explore some common obstacles prompters face and discuss strategies to overcome them. By understanding and addressing these challenges, you'll be better equipped to create effective prompts and achieve the desired outcomes.

1. Ambiguity and Lack of Clarity

One of the most common challenges prompters encounter is ambiguity and lack of clarity in prompts. When a prompt is unclear, it can lead to misunderstandings and generate inaccurate responses. To address this challenge, consider the following techniques: - Be specific: Clearly define the context and objectives of the prompt. Use precise language and provide detailed instructions to guide the AI model. - Use examples: Incorporate relevant examples in your prompts to illustrate the expected output. These examples can help the AI model understand the desired response better. - Iterate and refine: Experiment with different phrasing and wording in your prompts. Test them to ensure they convey the intended meaning accurately.

2. Bias and Stereotyping

AI models can inadvertently produce biased or stereotypical

responses based on the prompts they receive. Addressing bias and stereotyping is a crucial challenge for prompters. Here are a few strategies to mitigate this issue: - Diversify prompts: Include prompts that represent a wide range of perspectives and experiences. This can help the AI model learn from diverse inputs and reduce the chances of biased outputs. - Review and analyze outputs: Regularly review and analyze the responses generated by the AI model. Identify any biases or stereotypes that may have surfaced and adjust your prompts accordingly. - Collaborate with AI developers: Work closely with the developers of the AI platform to address bias and improve the overall performance of the system.

3. Generating Coherent Responses

Another challenge prompters face is generating coherent and relevant responses from the AI model. Sometimes, the output may seem fragmented or unrelated to the prompt. To handle this challenge, consider the following techniques: - Contextual prompts: Provide sufficient context in your prompts to guide the AI model's response. Include relevant information that helps the model understand the prompt's purpose and requirements. - Experiment with prompt structure: Try different prompt structures to elicit more focused and coherent responses. You can break down complex queries into smaller, more manageable components. - Iterative refinement: Iterate on your prompts based on the feedback received from analyzing responses. Continuously refine and improve your prompts to enhance the coherence of the generated output.

4. Controlling Output Length

AI models often have a tendency to generate excessively long or short responses, which may not align with the desired outcome. To tackle this challenge, consider the following techniques: - Specify desired output length: Clearly indicate the desired length of the response in your prompts. This helps guide the AI model to generate output that meets the desired requirements. - Experiment with system and temperature settings: Adjusting the temperature setting can influence the level of randomness in the output. Experiment with different settings to find the balance that suits your needs. - Post-processing and truncation: Apply post-processing techniques to trim or expand the generated response as needed. Truncate lengthy outputs or add relevant additional information to shorter ones. By being aware of these common prompt challenges and implementing appropriate strategies, you can enhance the effectiveness of your prompts on AI platforms. Remember to continuously learn and adapt your prompt writing techniques to optimize the outcomes achieved through the collaboration with AI models.

CHAPTER 9:
OPTIMIZING PROMPT
PERFORMANCE

Optimizing prompt performance is a crucial aspect of prompt writing for AI platforms. It involves fine-tuning your prompts to ensure that you get the most accurate and desirable responses from the AI model. In this chapter, we will explore various techniques and strategies to optimize prompt performance and improve the quality of the generated output.

1. Understand the AI Model

To optimize prompt performance, it is essential to have a thorough understanding of the AI model you are working with. Familiarize yourself with its strengths, limitations, and common pitfalls. By understanding the underlying mechanisms of the model, you can tailor your prompts to leverage its capabilities effectively.

2. Experimentation is Key

Optimizing prompt performance often requires experimentation. Don't be afraid to try different approaches, structures, and wording in your prompts. Experimentation allows you to identify the most effective strategies that yield the desired results. Keep a record of your experiments and analyze the outcomes to refine your prompt writing process.

3. Test and Iterate

Testing and iterating your prompts is crucial to improving performance. Start with small tests, and gradually increase the complexity and specificity of the prompts. Analyze the responses and make adjustments accordingly. By iterating your prompts, you can fine-tune them to produce better results.

4. Leverage Prompt Engineering Techniques

Prompt engineering involves making modifications to prompts to achieve the desired output. Techniques such as providing context, specifying output formats, using temperature and max tokens, and utilizing system messages can greatly impact prompt performance. Experiment with different prompt engineering techniques to optimize the generated responses.

5. Analyze and Refine

Analyzing the responses generated by the AI model is crucial for optimizing prompt performance. Examine both the content and structure of the generated output. Identify any areas where the model produces inaccurate or nonsensical responses. Refine your prompts accordingly to minimize such issues.

6. Collaborate with AI trainers

Prompt writers should collaborate closely with AI trainers to optimize prompt performance. Share your findings, experiments, and challenges with the trainers, who can provide insights and guidance on improving your prompts. This collaboration helps ensure that the model's responses align with the intended objectives.

7. Regularly Update Prompt Library

Prompt writers should constantly update their prompt library based on feedback and insights gained from prompt performance optimization. As you learn more about the AI model and experiment with different strategies, incorporate successful prompts into your library. Regular updates ensure that you have a robust collection of prompts that consistently yield high-quality responses. In conclusion, optimizing prompt performance is a continuous process that involves understanding the AI model, experimentation, testing, prompt engineering, analysis, collaboration, and regular updates to the prompt library. By implementing the techniques discussed in this chapter, prompt writers can enhance the quality and accuracy of the generated output, ultimately improving the overall user experience on AI platforms.

www.ingramcontent.com/pod-product-compliance
Lightning Source LLC
LaVergne TN
LVHW051651050326
832903LV00034B/4809